Zen paths to Laughter

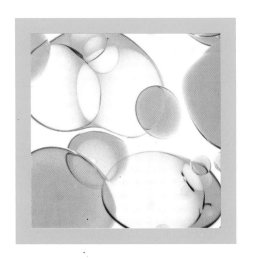

Zen paths to Laughter

Journey Editions
Boston • Tokyo • Singapore

Introduction

Laughter uplifts the spirit. Like a flash, it appears from nowhere to illuminate a dull day. Even at moments of great sadness we need laughter, which is why it often emerges when people are brought together in grief. As the quotation from George Bernard Shaw on page 90 reads: "Life does not cease to be funny when people die any more than it ceases to be serious when people laugh." Laughter is a way of easing the pain that is a reality of life. It brings balance, a release of tension, and thus calm.

Zen asks us to adopt a youthful attitude to life, to see it as it is, rather than as we want it to be. In this way we experience our lives more vividly. Often, comedians play on this in their routines. Their acute observations highlight the absurdity of some of our attitudes and customs. Because the words of comedians are so true, we can laugh with each other at ourselves. This is why you will find the names of some great comedians within the pages of this book.

Laughter can come from anywhere. It erupts because it exposes the real. With it comes a reminder of the joy of being alive and the companionship of friends and family. This book reveals some of the myriad sources of laughter, and accompanies them with natural and conceptual images.

If you wish to glance inside a human soul
and get to know a man...
just watch him laugh.
If he laughs well, he's a good man.

Fyodor Dostoyevsky

The Way is really rather exasperating.

R. H. Blyth

Even when freshly washed

and relieved of all obvious confections,

children tend to be sticky.

Fran Lebowitz

There are only two things a child will share willingly—

communicable diseases

and his mother's age.

Dr. Benjamin McLane Spock

"When I use a word,"
Humpty Dumpty said
in rather a scornful tone,
"it means just what
I **choose** it to mean—

neither
more
nor less."

Lewis Carroll

Time flies like an arrow,

fruit flies like a banana.

Groucho Marx

The most exciting phrase to hear in science,

the one that heralds the most discoveries,

is not **"Eureka!"**,

but "That's funny..."

Isaac Asimov

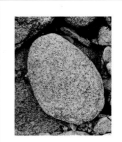

I am willing to admit
that I may not always be **right**,
but I am never wrong.

Samuel Goldsmith

Those are my **principles**.
If you don't like them
I have others.

Groucho Marx

You can learn many things from children.

How much **patience** you have, for instance.

Franklin P. Adams

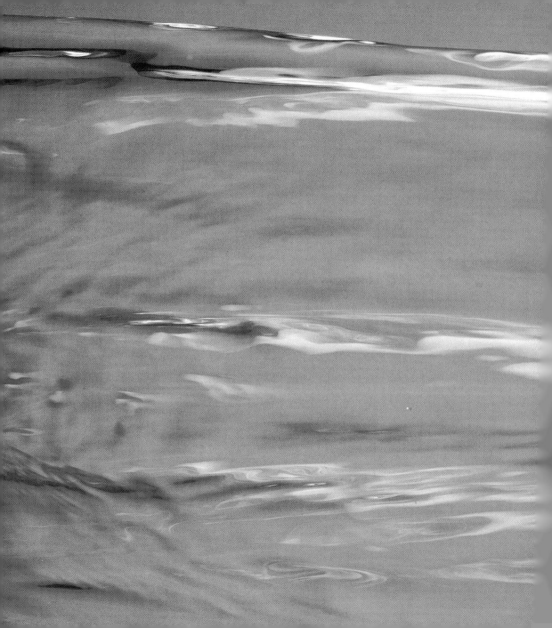

There's a **fine line** between fishing

and standing on the shore like an idiot.

Steven Wright

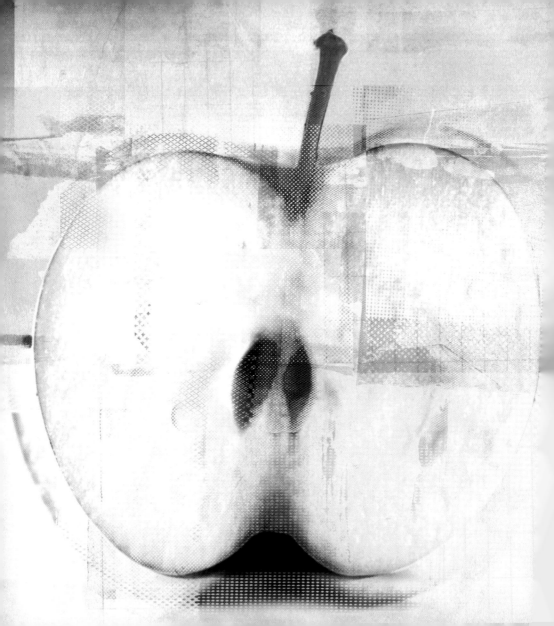

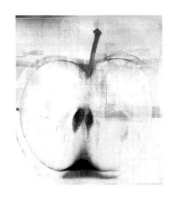

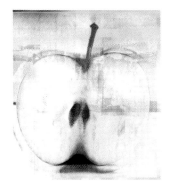

Gravitation

cannot be held responsible

for people falling in love.

Albert Einstein

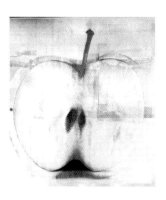

What makes equality such a difficult business is that we only want it with our superiors.

Henry Becque

I don't mind living in a **man's** world

as long as I can be a woman in it.

Marilyn Monroe

A lady's imagination is very rapid;

it jumps from **admiration** to love,

from **love** to matrimony

in a moment.

Jane Austen

Room Service?
Send up a larger room.

Groucho Marx

My **childhood** should have taught me lessons

for my own **parenthood**,

but it didn't

because parenting can be learned only

by people who **have no children**.

Bill Cosby

If you follow all the **rules**, you miss all the fun.

Katharine Hepburn

I play John Wayne in every picture
regardless of the character,
and I've been doing all right,
haven't I?

John Wayne

It is **easier** to get
an actor to be a **cowboy**
than to get a cowboy
to be an actor.

attributed to John Ford

I'm astounded by people

who want to "know" the universe

when it's hard enough

to find your way around Chinatown.

Woody Allen

I have an existential map:

it has

"you are here"

written all over it.

Steven Wright

If you have to tell them **who you are**,

you aren't anybody.

Gregory Peck

I am very interested in the universe—

I am *specializing* in the universe

and all that surrounds it.

Peter Cook

If a word in the dictionary were misspelled,

how would we know?

Steven Wright

Don't worry about the
world coming to an end
today.
It's already

tomorrow

in Australia.

Charles Schulz

Before I was married,

I had a **hundred** theories about raising children

and no children.

Now, I have three children

and **no** theories.

John Wilmot, Earl of Rochester

Middle age is when you've met so many people

that every **new** person you meet

reminds you of

someone else.

Ogden Nash

Life's too short for chess.

Henry James Byron

I have made this letter longer than usual, only because I have not had the time to make it shorter.

Blaise Pascal

You can't have **everything**.

Where would you put it?

Steven Wright

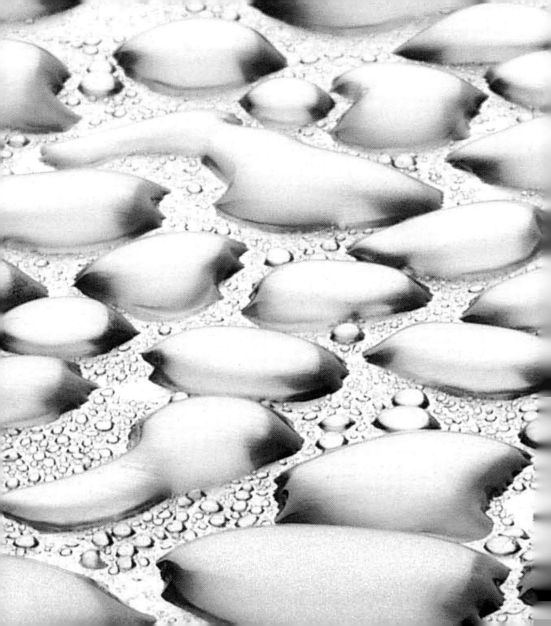

Give me a laundry-list

and I'll set it to music.

Gioacchino Rossini

If you treat
a sick child
like an **adult**
and a sick adult
like a **child**,
everything usually
works out pretty well.

Black Hawk

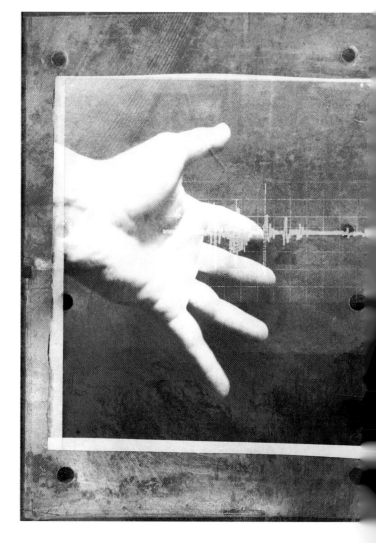

S₃

Space is almost infinite.

As a matter of fact
we think it is infinite.

Dan Quayle

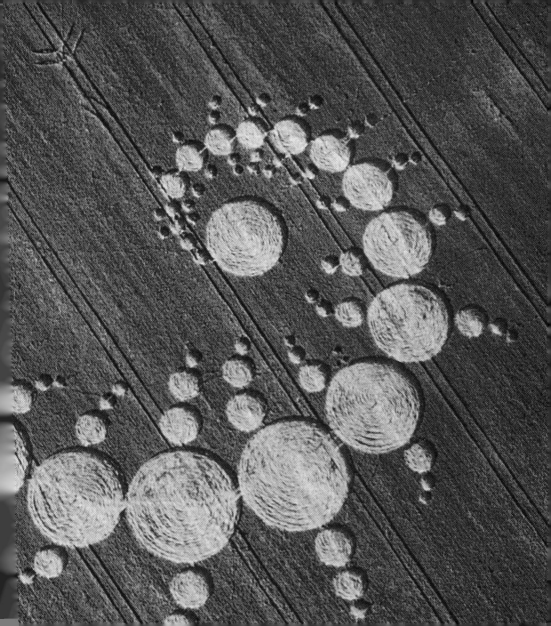

I'll give you a **definite** maybe.

Samuel Goldsmith

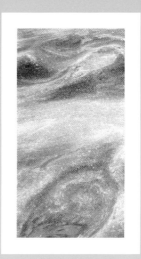

Human beings are
the **only** creatures
that allow their children
to come back home.

Bill Cosby

Tragedy

is if I cut my finger.

Comedy

is if I walk into an open sewer

and die.

Mel Brooks

Oh, to be seventy again!

Oliver Wendel Holmes, Jr

Thank heavens the sun has gone in
and I don't have to go out and enjoy it.

attributed to Logan Pearsall Smith

I am an **atheist** still,

thank God.

Luis Bunuel

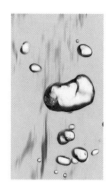

I am **dying** with the help of too many physicians.

Alexander the Great

I do really think that death will be marvellous...

If there wasn't death,

I think we couldn't go on.

Stevie Smith

Life does not cease to be funny

when people **die**

any more than it ceases to be serious

when people laugh.

George Bernard Shaw

I don't want to achieve **immortality**

through my work.

I want to achieve it

through **not dying.**

Woody Allen

Well, if I called the wrong number,

why did YOU answer the phone?

James Thurber

First published in the United States in 2000 by Journey Editions, an imprint of
Periplus Editions (HK) Ltd., with editorial offices at 153 Milk Street, Boston,
Massachusetts 02109.

Editor: Alison Moss
Series designer: Plum Partnership
Designer: Yvonne Dedman

Library of Congress Catalog Card Number: 00-105190

ISBN: 1582900418

First edition
06 05 04 03 02 01 00 10 9 8 7 6 5 4 3 2 1

Printed in Italy

Distributed by

NORTH AMERICA	JAPAN	ASIA PACIFIC
Tuttle Publishing	Tuttle Publishing	Berkeley Books Pte Ltd
Distribution Center	RK Building, 2nd Floor	5 Little Road 08-01
Airport Industrial Park	2-12-10 Shimo-Meguro	Singapore 536983
364 Innovation Drive	Meguro-Ku	Tel: (65) 280-1330
North Clarendon	Tokyo 153 0064	Fax: (65) 280-6290
VT 05759-9436	Tel: (03) 5437-0171	
Tel: (802) 773-8930	Fax: (03) 5437-0755	
Fax: (800) 526-2778